Your Gentle Heart is a Warrior

Poems on Survival and Healing

Sohini Trehan

BookLeaf Publishing

India | USA | UK

Presentation by *BookLeaf Publishing*

Web: www.bookleafpub.com

E-mail: info@bookleafpub.com

ISBN: 9789360942625

First edition 2024

Dedicated to all cycle breakers – for surviving, healing, and nurturing humanity

ACKNOWLEDGEMENT

In Honor of Shakti, who is my heart.

My ancestors, family, and parents who bless me every day.

My soul sister cycle breakers who inspire me.

To Tara, who lights my way, and Ashish, the guardian of my heart, this is for you.

Content Advisory – Some of the poems in this book make references to mental health, generational trauma, gender disparity, loss, and grief. Readers who might be sensitive to these aspects, please take note. Reading about these topics can bring up emotions and memories, and it is very important to remember to use the journal prompts to acknowledge and give space for these feelings and that it's always safe to seek the support of a mental health professional during and after difficult life situations.

CONTENTS

Introduction.. 13

The Invitation.. 1

The Empath's Heart.. 4

The Song of Life... 7

Holding Space... 11

Reunion... 14

All of a Kind.. 17

Brave.. 21

Notes From My Future Self.................................... 24

Grief is Love... 27

Our Father's Love.. 30

The Pain of Healing... 33

My Grandmother's Hands....................................... 37

An Incomplete List of Feminists in My Life............. 40

I Am Not My Trauma.. 43

Being in Love.. 46

Notes From a Therapist... 49

Gentle Reminders... 52

Dear Mother... 55

Belonging... 59

Heart to Heart... 62

We Save Each Other... 65

Inner Child... 67

Your Gentle Heart is a Warrior............................... 69

Closing Notes from the Author............................... 73

Introduction

If you were to decide one day to pause a few minutes and sit in the company of your own heart...what would it say? And more importantly, how would this heart-centred connection change you and your life?

If you were to sit with your heart every day for a few minutes and invite it to join you for a warm cup of tea, would it speak to you as a loving friend or would it converse with you as a wise mystic?

Would your heart fill your life up with its unending capacity for love and joy or would it flood you with its sensitivity, rawness, pain, and grief?

Would its gentleness inspire and strengthen you, or would it make you vulnerable and break you open?

Would its softness soothe your soul, or would its beating presence bring you back to a life of authentic healing?

Would this journey of "sitting with your heart" take you into the deepest and most fulfilling journey of this life where you become one with your gentle heart and show up as who you always were meant to be?

These simple yet evocative questions are at the core of this book of poems, where every page is an invitation for you to connect to your heart and know and live your unique truths. For if we are brave enough… when we show up in our lives, centred from our hearts, we finally understand that it's the one true warrior always on our side, the one who never abandons us in the battleground and the one who helps us survive, heal, and create an authentic life.

Our heart, this gentle warrior, just needs us to connect with it deeply so it can heal our wounds and carry us safely forward into the bravest yet most fulfilling journey of our lives… our heart is our unseen ally that supports us on every step of our journey through Life and when we establish a strong energetic connection with it… it's the gentle warrior that will empower us to truly live our best life.

The Invitation

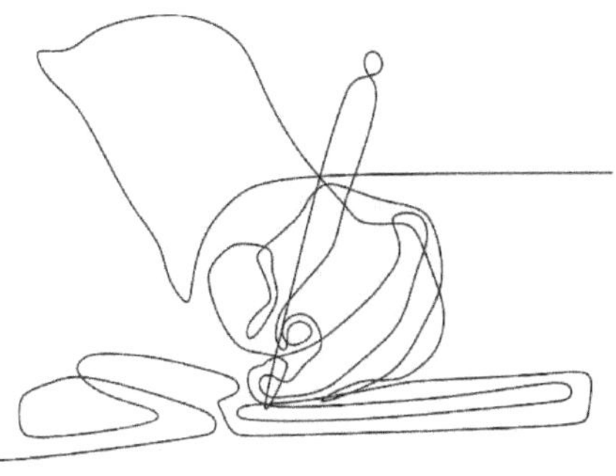

I sat down to write an invitation today
The pen in my hand waited
As minutes passed by
I knew I needed time
Time to ease out of thinking
Of the perfect words
To feel my emotions
Softly I hugged myself
And wrote again
Dear heart, this feels awkward
That I am inviting you
A part of me
Such a precious part
To sit down over a cup of tea
I want to be fully alive and present
With you my heart

As I sat in the awkwardness
Of my feelings I felt a soft voice moving up
From the centre of my being
Thank you for seeing me
My heart said
I have been waiting
For this invitation all my life
Thank you
For your presence
So we can be whole
I put down my pen
And placed my hands
Over my heart again
And it embraced me back
With a soft gentle sigh
We were finally together
And at that moment
I realised I was never alone

Have you ever spoken to your heart and has your heart spoken back to you? Take a deep breath and ask your heart what it is feeling at this moment and write down its answers here…

The Empath's Heart

Are you tired of feeling too much
Of noticing more than most around you
Of sensing everyone's pain
Of not feeling sure where you end
And others' emotions begin
You dear human are a deep feeler
With a rich inner life of emotions
A dreamer of love and no wars
Things, names and accomplishments
Don't matter to you
What matters is how life moves you
And if you are able to make a difference
Are you also tired of people telling you
To be strong and are you numbed out
By the sting of words asking you
For taking things too seriously
Do you also wish you could harden yourself
And just stop with the awareness
Of all that exists

I feel you and I hold space
For all of you but I want to tell you
Dear empath, never change
Having a soft heart
In a hard world is deeply and desperately needed
You are needed
So stay you and protect your heart
Make a difference but rest more
Hold space for people but with boundaries
Be open to life but say no too
Be you and guard your beautiful heart
And self preciously
Don't ever barter your introvert self
For the loud head-tripping demands of the world
Never apologize for your gentle heart
Never gaslight your empath parts
And if you find yourself doing so
Which we are all guilty of
Remind yourself that you are
What you need and what the world needs
Hold yourself as softly as possible
Dear empath
Because everytime you do
There is another being with a soft heart
Who feels seen and belonged and needed
Because of you

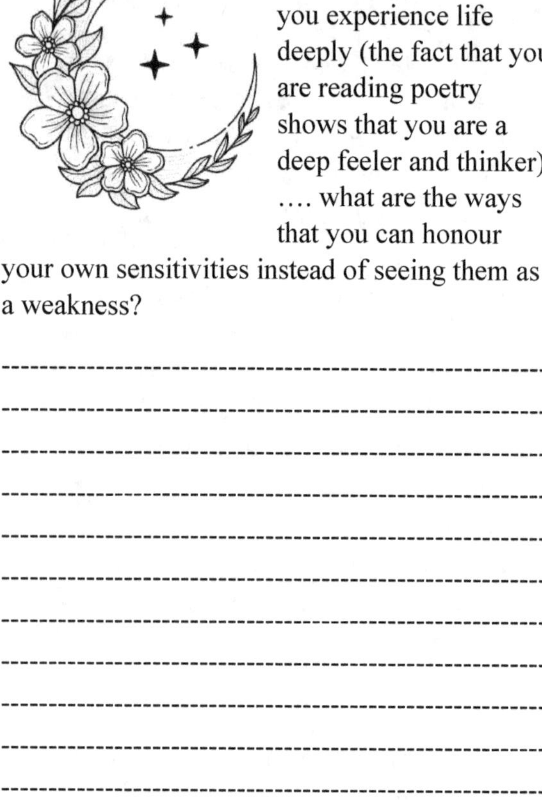

Have you been called sensitive by people? Do you experience life deeply (the fact that you are reading poetry shows that you are a deep feeler and thinker) …. what are the ways that you can honour your own sensitivities instead of seeing them as a weakness?

The Song of Life

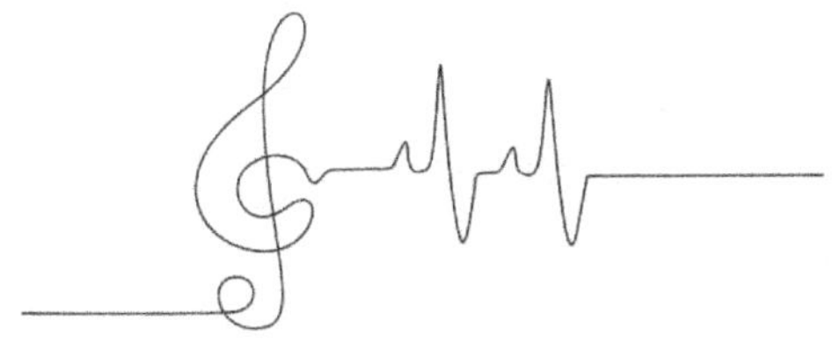

When do we first start hearing sounds
Do they start gathering around us
In our fetal journey
As we grow in our mother's womb
The hums and echoes of words and sounds of
Conversations between people and voices
Speaking to us
Birds chirping, machines whirring
The sounds of the world
Or is it the woosh of our mother's heart
The very first sound we hear
A song of rhythmic heartbeats
That embraces us and makes us
Feel safe and loved
As our ears form and pick up noises
From the outside world
Some soothing, others startling
Does the steady rhythm of the heart
Become our very first music

Sitting around a drum circle when I
Move into a trance where my body just
Relaxes and sighs with ease
I understand finally
That this primitive music was the very first one
This drum beat feels familiar and safe to my
Body and takes me back
To a fetal memory which I cannot
Verbalise and express but only feel
That my body is reliving a memory
That my mind cannot recall
A memory where the heart's beating was the
Very first sound she heard
As my beautiful being began to take
A human form and shape
Preparing for birth
As I was serenaded by my mother's heart
And as my own embryonic heart grew stronger
With this safe and soothing rhythm
The song of life strung together
From one womb to another
Becoming the song
Of our ancestors and successors
Carrying a million notes
Of love, grief and joy
Immeasurable songs within every heartbeat
Of heartbreaks and celebrations
Infinite songs of our humanness
Connecting us irrevocably

To the cosmic heartbeat
The beating of my mother's heart
Which was serenaded by my grandmother
And so it continues backwards and forwards
As I now hold the legacy of this sacred rhythm
So when do we first start hearing sounds?
As I revisit this exploration with the deepest
Most profound answers lying open within me
I find myself content and at ease
Not to think or verbalise this knowing
Into neat little streams of rational thoughts
And words
But just to feel this sacred knowing
That before we even start hearing sounds
Before we even learn how to connect
And communicate
We already are
Deeply, solidly and eternally connected
To people, to nature and to all of life itself
That's the only truth of my belonging
The only reason I will ever need for my
Enough-Ness

Does music move you deeply… have you healed through music? Take a moment to remember a time when you truly felt the power of music in your life…

Holding Space

The most beautiful people
Are the ones who have created
So much of space within themselves
Where they have birthed
A new kind of compassion
One that is totally different from
What the world sees as compassion
This kind is all theirs
They created within moments
And days and years when they
Yearned for love and connection
And belonging and validation
But did not receive it because
They slowly realised that it was
Not anybody else's to give
But for themselves to create
The most beautiful people
Are the ones who are on a journey
Of creating their own version of self-love

And nurturing their own meaning
Of self-compassion
Where they understand that inner peace
Doesn't come but lives and breathes
Where there is room for all our parts
The parts that are happy and
The parts that are sad
The parts that are healed and the
Parts that are wounded
The parts that are worthy and the
Parts that are angry
Because they know
That all these parts
Are the ones that love
Them the most
The most beautiful people
Are the ones that have made peace
With living and holding space
For all of themselves

Do you believe that true peace and healing come through sitting with our feelings? What does self-compassion mean to you?

Reunion

Today I looked in the mirror
And paused as I saw myself
Realising it had been weeks
Since the last time our eyes met
In the rush of the days gone by
Everytime I looked in the mirror
It was to check if I looked okay
To fix or add or adjust
To apply or adorn
To feel good or judge
But today when I looked in the mirror
As I softly brushed my hair
Our eyes finally met after so long
Like lost pieces of the same heart
Finally in a space
Where they don't have to be
Anything but themselves
Knowing that they love

And are loved
Unconditionally
So today I looked in the mirror
And met myself
I saw me and I sighed
Smiled and paused
To say what the mirror has been
Craving to hear
"I love you "
I say softly
"I truly deeply love you
I might forget to say this
And I want to do this more often
I want to do this everyday
I love you
I am so proud of you
Of the mountains and valleys
You have journeyed
I love you
For your resilience
I love you for your compassion
I love you
And I love you the most
Amongst everyone I love"
And I saw my eyes smile
As they pooled up
And my face glowed magically
And I stepped into the sunshine
Feeling beautiful like never before

Are you able to see yourself eye to eye? Start with a few seconds and some words of love. It's not an easy process but you might just fall in love with your own self eventually. Write down a few non-physical compliments for yourself here that you can recall during your own reunion.

All of a Kind

She is
The kind of woman
Who converses deeply
Who thinks even more deeper
Who is vulnerable yet strong
Who is sweet yet savage
She is
The kind of woman
Who needs a lot
A lot of nature
A lot of alone time
A lot of self-compassion
A lot of love
She is
The kind of woman

Who feels a lot
A lot of rage
A lot of grief
A lot of joy
A lot of empathy
She is
The kind of woman
Who is healing and grieving
Who survived
But was never a victim
Who lost but was never defeated
Who sees fellow women
Really sees them
Who holds space for her sisters
Who lifts others up
And cheers them on
She is
The kind of woman
Who is growing everyday
Who knows what she wants
Who is shedding all the parts
That were never her own
She is
A medicine woman
A wounded healer
She is your ancestor
She is your successor
Your mother
Your daughter

And She is YOU
Beating deep within
Supporting you
Cheering you
Protecting you
And waiting for you
To take this brave journey
With her
The only journey of this life
That ever counts
The journey of
Living your truth
Of knowing who you are
The journey from surviving
To messy healing
And authentic living
She is the kind of woman
Who all women are born to be
Who all women are becoming
At their unique pace
With their unique struggles
She is the kind of woman
Who understands that
Every woman is leading
Every woman home

If you were to show up fully as yourself in your life, what would that look like?

Brave

She feels at home around the tallest trees
Most of all when the morning sun shines
She breathes deeper and laughs fuller
And walks softly, really tenderly
So her feet can taste the ground
She was born brave
A rebel who never learnt
The ways of the world
But under the moon and the stars
Among the trees and the grass
Soaked in sunshine and rain
Is the place that she calls home
The only place where
She is welcomed fully
With deep love
Where she can

Shed all the roles
And worthiness
And just be loved
And feel belonging
Because she is alive

Does nature soothe you? What are some soft ways by which you connect with nature and how would you like to deepen this bond?

Notes From My Future Self

Thank you
Broken one
Brave one
Beautiful one
For pausing
For being so brave

When you looked scattered to the world
In reality it was you being vulnerable
When you looked still to the world
In reality you allowed yourself rest
And Self-compassion
When you seemed withdrawn from the world
In reality you were just learning the real
Meaning of self-care
When you looked angry to the world
In reality you were just creating boundaries for
Your self-preservation
When you became too negative for the world
In reality you were trying to sit with your
Feelings so you could heal
Thank you dearest one
For being so brave
For allowing yourself to feel
Thank you for giving me
And our children the freedom

To be more free and more of
Who we really are and
Not what the world sees us to be
Thank you for not conforming
To society's flawed standards
Of living and thriving
They know not what is real
Thank you for being at peace
With your authentic self and
Choosing yourself everyday
For being so brave everyday
For I your future know
How brave you are going to be

"In order to truly create a desirable future we cannot live in denial of our present"

When you think of an older version of yourself, what do you envision? Write down some words that would describe your future self…

Grief is Love

Grief and Love met each other one day
Never knowing that the time had come
To walk together for the rest of their lives
Love asked Grief if he could hold her hand
She was not sure, but nodded softly
And embraced Love
For Grief understood now that they could
Never exist without each other
She was proof of Love's eternal existence
As much as his non–physical absence
And Love was everything that is life and beyond
Even when he did not feel alive or needed
He tenaciously held on
And survived through grief
Each of them growing together with grace
Homed in our hearts to remind us of

The circle of life and death
Births and passings
Pain and healing
Grief and Love
Meeting and merging into one
When it's time to unite
And as we open our hearts
To make space for both of them
We begin one more time to truly
Understand what love is
Because Grief finally shows us
Love's true expanse and depth
As we grow through life's truth
That Love is Grief
And Grief is Love living on

How has losing a loved one changed your understanding of grief and love in your life?

Our Father's Love

Our father loved like no one else
And though he has passed away
His love and light stays on
Like fireflies in the void that
Has opened up in his physical absence
Our father's love was beautifully vocal
For that I am deeply grateful
For we never had to look for signs
And validations that he loved
He always said so often
In words that were reassuring
How much he was proud of us
How much he loved us
How much he cherished us
We were always our father's children
That was enough to earn his love
Nothing more
I wonder often now
How much love it took
For him to put aside his own pain

And not let anything but
Love and light come through
My Father's Love
Was like no one else's
And we deeply miss him
While I know he lives on
Through his incomparable love
And ours

"A father's soft, gentle love has the power of breaking down generations of patriarchy"

Do you feel it is important for men to be expressive and in touch with their emotional and sensitive parts?

The Pain of Healing

You asked me the other day
Why is healing so painful
When all you thought was
That this journey would
Soothe and take away the pain
And I sighed and said
You know you are healing now
Because healing is never the balm
But more painful than the wounding itself
Because healing needs so much of us
Because while the wounding can eventually
Numb us
Healing awakens us with
Breaking us down
Cracking our parts open

And releasing the grief
It's all life-consuming
But when the body asks for healing
We can never bypass its pain anymore
She asks us to listen
And when we honor her
She begs us to sit with us
She tells us it's enough
She cannot take being
Not at home in her being
She wants to feel loved by us
Not hatred or craving for love
From the ghosts of past caretakers and lovers
It will never be enough even if
They return or change or accept us
What she needs is us to sit
With our bodies because it's
Not just a body of skin and hair and bones
The body is the heart, the soul and the spirit and
the mind and all of it needs healing
We let a sigh and are deeply scared
What this sitting with our body will bring
How much will it want us to crack open
And we begin nevertheless feeling scared
And our body sighs for the first time in our lives
which feels like rest
And she says ...I know how scary it is ..but
This is the bravest we have ever been
And now that we are numb no more

We are healing
Feeling is painful
And feeling is healing
So will this pain lessen ever
You ask me with hope and longing
For a time when you could just
Live days of joyful presence
And I softly hold your hand
And say
Yes the pain lessens
Slowly and cautiously as we
Fill up the wounds with
Self-care and love and
The softest of boundaries
Our bodies and spirits then
Finally heal knowing for sure
That she is home now,
Safe with you
Her most trusted Self

What does healing mean for you?

My Grandmother's Hands

My Grandmother's Hands
My first and forever love
She showed my heart
The true feeling of tenderness
When I think of her
Memories, moments, words
All somehow merge into one
Feeling within my heart
And a lump in my throat
The softness of her being
Is everything that is love
And her hands are what
Stay the clearest in my soul's memory
Her hands hold so many stories
Of a life lived with love
Stories of deaths and rebirths
Stories of joys and traumas

Stories of survival and strength
As my daughter asks me once again
To tell her more about my grandmother
I take her hands in mine and smile softly
Grateful for my first and forever love

Has an elderly person played a positive, loving role in your life during your childhood? Try to write down what that felt like…

An Incomplete List of Feminists in My Life

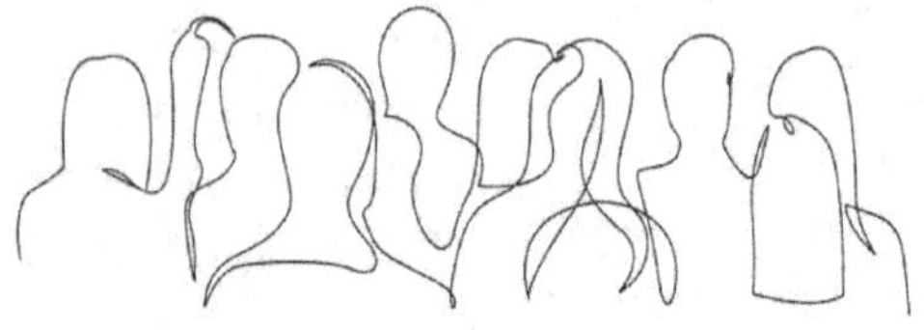

My Great Grandmother
For choosing to live with her daughter

My Grandmother
For studying hard, going to college and
becoming financially independent

My Mother
For making her own choices in life, love and
work

My Father
For loving me and my brother equally

My Partner
For creating an equal marriage

My Daughter
For taking up space fearlessly and rightfully

My Sister and Brother
For raising feminist daughters

My Best Friend
For breaking gender stereotypes

My Domestic Help
For working hard and proud as a single working
mother

My Neighbors
For supporting their daughter in her divorce

My Soul Family of All Gender Identities
For loving and treating each other equally with
empathy

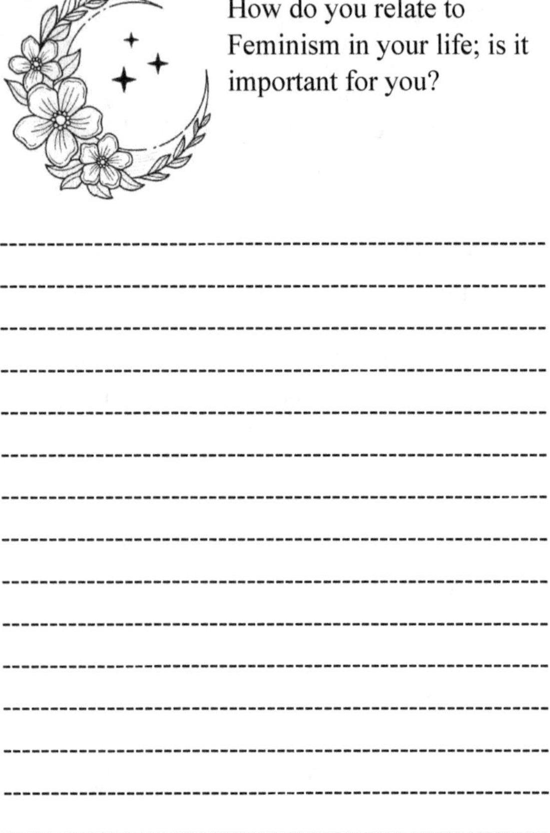

How do you relate to Feminism in your life; is it important for you?

I Am Not My Trauma

My trauma has shaped my emotions and
Responses to life
But I am not my trauma
My trauma has shaped how I speak to myself
But I am not my trauma
My trauma has shaped how I judge my body but
I am not my trauma
My Trauma has shaped my thoughts and
Judgements but I am not my trauma
My trauma has shaped how I show up in my
Relationships and this world
But I am not my trauma

I am not my trauma
I am not what happened to me
I am my being
I am my heart

I am my soul
I am my spirit
I am my life
I am my healing
I am the soft smile I smile
I am the tears of joy
I am the hug of compassion
I am the peace I feel in simple moments
I am the love I see in my eyes looking back at
Me in the mirror
I am not my trauma
I am free
I am me

Who is the safest person you know?

Being in Love

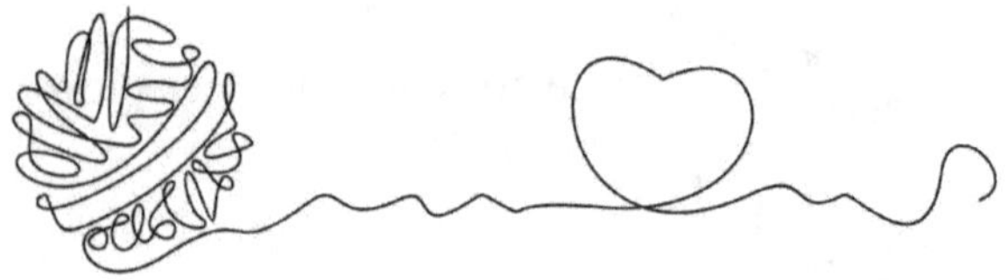

This being in love
Is effortless
Yet so much work
This being in love
As Lovers
Is magical yet so deeply vulnerable
This being in love as humans
Is healing and heartbreaking
This being in love as man and wife
Is a constant battle of creating equality
This being in love as parents
Is precious and messy
This being in love
Is our life and our way of being
Is forever yet a daily choice
To be kind and choose love
Everyday over the world
This being in love
Is a gift
That we hold
Tenderly and gratefully

Two beings in love
Living life kindly
Compassionately and consciously
Is our love in being

What is your love language?

Notes From a Therapist

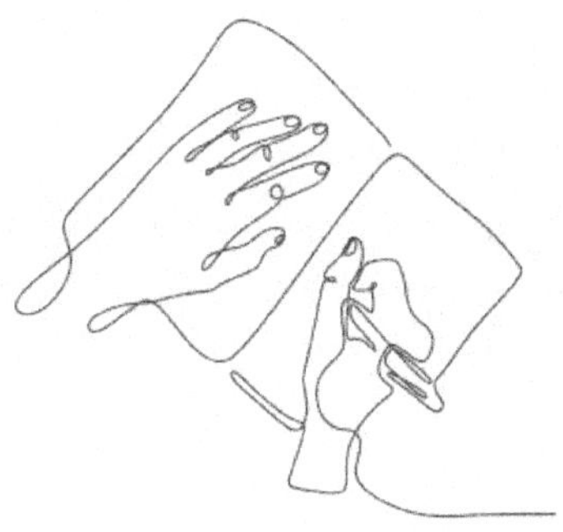

While you sat there feeling unsure
I sat across admiring you because in your
Vulnerability I saw the deep strength that would
Take you through so much reclamation in the
Coming years

While you sat there feeling undone
I sat across admiring you because having the
Power to sit with their shadow self is one of the
Greatest gifts we can ever give ourselves
Because all your parts that feel low just want
Your presence and you being able to do that is
Everything

While you sat there releasing your tears
I sat across admiring you because grief comes to
Us as proof of our many loves and lives lived,

Of losses and could have beens but I knew that
You would grow around this grief and the tears
And it would nourish you softly like morning
Rain on wildflowers

While you sat there talking awkwardly
I sat across admiring you because I heard you
Talking to your parts in the most gentlest and
Compassionate way and I had never seen
Anything as beautifully human as that moment.

While you sat there softly smiling at me
I sat there feeling unsure of my place across you
Because I finally knew you had found your way
Back home and it was my time to leave

Do you feel you are in tune with your emotions? At this moment try writing down five emotions you are feeling and try to identify where you feel them in your body…

Gentle Reminders

You are enough just as you are
There is so much time to be all of you
Go slow through today and rest more
Your beauty is immeasurable
Never judge it through societal standards
Try to be okay with being the villain
In some people's stories as long as
You have been there for yourself
Speak up, stand up for yourself
Everyday, every hour
You are never too much
Stop doing more for others
Use that time for yourself
To make up for the decades of
Sleep, nourishment and peace
You truly and deeply need
Soften all your guilts and self-loathings
Become your own best companion

Take yourself out for dates
Invest in yourself as much as possible
Heal because you deserve to thrive
Talk about what matters to you
Listen to your body's requests
Be proud of your journey
Remind yourself of your basic needs
Everyday so that slowly
You start taking space for yourself
In your life with all the care you deserve

What is one most important
self-care practice you
would love to do more
often?

Dear Mother

I am a lot like you
Yet so different
I have a strong mind of my own
Like you
And a soft heart like yours
Yet while you move with everyone together
I am the lone wolf who treads with caution
Sometimes I can see the questions in your eyes
About my boundaries and fierce love
For my own space
And how you try to understand them with grace
I am resilient like you
But more vulnerable and sensitive too
As it's your choices in life
That give me the privilege to
Become the woman I am today
Who chooses freedom over and over

To keep growing into a woman
Who chooses herself over and over
It is because of you
That I have learnt of love
In all shades of its darkest hues
To the most uplifting ones
It's because of your pain
That I have a soft ground to rest more
Because my heart and soul allow that
And I am able to be kinder to my parts
Than you could ever be
It's because of you that
I have created a life for me
So my daughter can always know
In her bones and sinews
All of her worth
Like I know because of you
Dear mother
Of course my heart is softer
My worth is deeper
My privileges are more
All because you handed
These better parts over to me
To nourish them safely
Our legacy which I
Pass on to my daughter
Who is the fiercest and kindest
Human I know
Who is wild and free

Because of your mother
Who despite her chains
Broke the shackles for her daughter
As you did for me
And now my daughter does
For herself, Dear Mother.

In what ways are you the same and different from your mother?

Belonging

When I look at the wildflowers
And sit in their divine presence
They soothe me and fill me up
With a joy that cannot be expressed
Their beingness is something
I crave for, because I see
That they know they just belong
These wildflowers came up
From the soil and spread their roots
And blossomed under the sun and moon
Just being and living in their belonging
As I sit in their presence this afternoon
I am filled with a wish for my daughter
I want to create spaces where she can
Blossom without conditional acceptance
I want her to follow the song of her heart

So that even when the world asks
For proofs and performances and decides
Her worth based on the broken
And oppressive blueprint of gender roles
She still feels worthy because she exists
And understands the value of never
Trading her true self for acceptability

Where do you truly feel at
home? Is it with a person or
a place?

Heart to Heart

I want to give my daughter
A forever space
Where she can be
All her parts
A forever space
To speak
To cry
To laugh
To speak out her innermost fears
And hopes
And while I want nothing in return
I can see that as this space builds
Between me and her
She allows me so much grace
To share my parts as well
Our hearts meet often

As she holds it tenderly
And I hold hers
Like I did my mother's
And she does mine

How do you feel in the company of children, is there a child in your life you share a connection with?

We Save Each Other

As long as we are living
In this web of life
My deepest anchor
For hope and grace
Is that we save each other
Everytime I try
To save myself
I am saving another
And everytime you
Try to support me
In saving myself
You save me and
Yourself as well
That's how healing happens
That's how transformation begins
That's how we save humanity
For nobody can save themselves
We save each other

"We are not really living unless we are serving humanity"

What is the most crucial value we need to practice in society as humans according to you?

Inner Child

Last night I dreamt
That I was a young girl
Once again
A girl of all ages
Shapeshifting into a toddler
Then an infant and a teenager
In my dream I was running
And singing and laughing
And I remember holding hands
And walking on soft green grass
With a beautiful soft woman
Who made me feel safe and held
I woke up feeling the joy and peace
Within my heart and it felt
Deeply familiar like the dream
I placed my hands over my heart
As I rocked myself in bed
And my heart whispered
You are whole
She is free
And happy and safe and held
Within you and by you
Beautiful soft one

What are the ways by which you can connect with your inner child?

Your Gentle Heart is a Warrior

Dear Heart
All these years while I was
Growing
Surviving
Healing
Living
Fighting
Crying
Supporting
Feeling
Giving up
Rising again
Standing up
Giving back
Breathing
Resting

Setting Boundaries
Empathetically engaging
Nurturing
Asking
Showing up
Saying no
Listening
Holding space
Taking up space
Loving
Creating Change
Questioning
Rebelling
Coming out of my comfort zone
Going back in for my self-preservation
Through this all
Again and again
With every cycle
Opening and closing
Please know that
While wanting to
Live free
At peace and
With all the respect
You truly deserve
You are my warrior
And savior and
I am always safe
As long as I dance

My own dance of life
To the beats of my gentle heart
...My Warrior

Do you listen to your heart and follow through with its guidance? What does it tell you today?

Closing Notes from the Author

I have always found peace and grounding through writing, especially intuitive free verse, where the poems form themselves as I witness the expression of my parts. Stream-of-consciousness writing, which is writing without censure about whatever comes through the heart, feels deeply cathartic to my senses, almost like a release and reset. The words bring me back to my body and also help me softly remember my place in this thing called life. And while I never did or ever will consider myself a poet, I do know about this thing called life and surviving life because every day I hold space for humans and witness their extraordinary capacity to survive and heal.

Being a mental health counsellor, I am deeply inspired by the power and sheer resilience of the human spirit to survive and heal. Holding space for those who trust me vulnerably with their trauma and challenges has been a profoundly humbling human experience for me. Year after year, I stand in awe of the empowering ritual of healing that unfolds in people who are able to reclaim their lives once they feel safe and seen. From survival, they slowly move into heart-centred living and regain a deep-rooted sense of love and belonging for themselves.

Witnessing my precious circle of people acknowledging their trauma, working through it all and embracing their most authentic versions makes me feel so very grateful for the privilege of holding space for them. I feel that every poem on these pages is mine and theirs. Not a single poem is perfect, either in prose or word choice, because their raw edges are what make me feel alive and real, and I hope some words or verses do the same for you.

If there was one truth that I have lived and relived by witnessing people heal from grief and trauma, including myself, it is this – the power of connecting to ourselves is life-changing and a necessity. We have to lean into ourselves every day. We have to create space to sit with our feelings and move away from our thoughts into our hearts – the feeler and speaker of all that is raw and real. The journal prompts after every poem are also an invitation from me to help you ease into your heart-centredness and lean more into yourself, especially at times when the demands of the world make you feel too fragmented. It is my wish that during such times, may you find your way back home through the free verses and by dipping into your own stream-of-consciousness writing.

Over the years studying with Dr Judith Orloff (psychiatrist), Dr Elaine Aron (Clinical Research Psychologist), Dr Richard Schwartz (Systemic Family Counsellor), Dr Gabor Mate (Childhood Developmental Therapist), Dr Peter Levine (Psychotraumatologist), Dr Manuella Mischke Reeds(Somatic Psychotherapist), Dr Marsha Linehan (Dialectical Behaviour Therapist) and several other mentors have helped and guided me in my personal life and professional practice to deepen my own experiential wisdom of healing and how several factors like genetics, gender, childhood experiences, cultural and social environments overlap with each other and deeply impact every individual's ability to process and respond to life. I have also understood that sensitivity and empathy go hand in hand with most people who are trying to heal through their life challenges and find true meaning and belonging in their lives.

Empathetic people have so much to be grateful for, mainly because they have the innate capacity to truly experience the poetry of life. Our capacity to witness the joy and beauty of life is rare. And our compassion gives us the power to help others in deeply meaningful ways. We are never emotionally unavailable or uncaring, and we feel a kinship with all of life. Nature moves us, and we feel connected to animals, flowers and trees in a surreal way. We can feel the soft earth beneath our feet and can commute with the energy of the wind, rain, sun, moon and stars with true belonging. The vastness of the oceans and the serenity of the mountains make our hearts expand and ground us in ways we can never express. Sensitive people also possess the maximum power to create positive change in the world. They are the ones who mostly break generations of rigid patterns of trauma in families, relationships and workplaces by becoming more conscious children, parents, colleagues and mentors.

Conscious healing is a lot of hard work. It's messy and exhausting. Is it worth it? Of course, it is. Only when people accept themselves for who they are, are they able to heal and also honor their soft parts by saying no to abuse and neglect and setting strong and healthy inner and outer boundaries. Self-care is something that should be taken up as a necessity. And one can be on a lifelong journey to explore which self-care practices make one feel deeply whole and grounded. For me, the simplest self-care rituals have been the most powerful. Soulful, heart-centred connections with my loved ones, deep conversations, lots of time in nature, playtime and fun with children, making nourishing meals for myself, gardening, connecting with self through silence and of course, writing poetry and journaling.

Over the span of the last twelve years, my work in the field of mental health service and recovery has considerably deepened, mainly because I have been able to work with my clients beyond the labels of mental health disorders and neurodevelopmental conditions so that together we could understand their trauma and its conscious and subconscious impacts on their mental, emotional, and physical states. And this was never because of my capacity as their therapist but their ability to heal in a safe space where they could just allow all their parts to exist and feel, especially their deeply sensitive and vulnerable parts. Every time I hold a soft space for another human, I feel deeply inspired and strengthened at the sheer valour and beauty of their gentle hearts – their one true warrior.

I am forever grateful to every person who is consciously trying to be emotionally available to themselves through whatever support that is possible for them. Because how we connect to ourselves matters. How we feel matters. And, feeling our feelings matter. It impacts our brains and body connection deeply and irrevocably. For the degree of our connection or disconnection to our own selves influences all areas of our lives, especially the ones where we feel we are failing at. Because every time I have witnessed a client or a loved one face their emotions and honor their sensitivities, I have always seen them heal, go through a rebirth and reclaim their lives in the best ways possible. So if there is one thing that I know, I know it's this – that the people who are actively healing are the strongest and bravest ones in the world and are also the most effective agents of change in our society. It is my most sincere wish that may these poems remind you of your belonging in this world and how much your healing journey impacts the world and people around you. My life's prayer is only one – may every gentle heart find its way back home and feel safe enough to heal and live a deeply fulfilling and authentic life.

Sohini Trehan

yourgentleheartisawarrior@gmail.com

9 789360 942625